# THE OFFICIAL AIR BRAKE HANDBOOK

This handbook is only a guide. For official purposes, please refer to the Ontario Highway Traffic Act and regulations. This handbook should not be used as a guide for repairs, which should only be carried out by a qualified person.

Disponible en français
Demandez le «Guide officiel de l'utilisation des freins à air»

MOMTAZ ZADEGAN

**Driving is a privilege—not a right**

Y0-BZI-586

# Contents

# Forward

This Official Air Brake Handbook has been written to help you safely operate a vehicle with air brakes and to help you recognize and prevent potential problems through a pre-trip inspection. It is designed to assist you in preparing for the Ministry of Transportation of Ontario's Air Brake Endorsement examination(s).

The Official Air Brake Handbook contains basic information about vehicles with air brakes. It does not cover every possible part and design for each type of vehicle system. Any maintenance information contained within this handbook is included only to help you better understand an air brake system. You are by no means encouraged to perform any service maintenance. This should be performed by a qualified person.

To help you remember what you read in this handbook, here are two tips:

1. Read this handbook as if you were going to explain what you have read to someone else.
2. Use the illustrations in this handbook as a guide to your reading.

# WHY YOU NEED AN AIR BRAKE ENDORSEMENT & RESPONSIBILITY FOR SAFETY

## Overview

This chapter contains information about:

1. Ontario's Air Brake ("Z") Endorsement.
2. The Canadian Motor Vehicle Safety Standards (CMVSS 121).
3. Air Brakes and Responsibility for Safety.

## Ontario's Air Brake ("Z") Endorsement

The Province of Ontario passed a bill requiring all drivers of vehicles with air brakes to become endorsed by the Ministry of Transportation of Ontario. You obtain this "Z" endorsement from the Ministry of Transportation of Ontario. This Air Brake Handbook contains all the information you will need to pass the "Z" endorsement test(s).

# Why You Need an Air Brake Endorsement & Responsibility for Safety

### Canadian Motor Vehicle Safety Standards (CMVSS 121)

This standard, commonly referred to as CMVSS 121, is a Federal Government standard for the manufacturers of air brake equipped vehicles. It came into effect in 1975.

The intent of the standard is to upgrade the air brake system and to reduce the incidence of emergency application of the vehicle's brakes due to system failure. This is accomplished by the introduction of a dual air brake system.

There is also a requirement that if one of the two systems fails, the emergency system must be able to bring the vehicle to a stop. This standard requires separate braking systems for service, emergency and parking. Another requirement is that there must be a parking brake control on a truck or a tractor, that controls the parking brakes of both the towing motor vehicle and any trailer(s) in tow.

### Air Brakes and Responsibility for Safety

If you are driving a vehicle equipped with air brakes, it is important to know about the entire air brake system and how to inspect it. It is also important to know what to expect when something goes wrong with your air brakes. You are responsible for the safe operation of the vehicle you drive. To help ensure safety, do a pre-trip inspection of the vehicle before you drive it.

# FACTORS THAT AFFECT BRAKING

## Overview

This chapter contains information about:
1. How air brakes compare with hydraulic brakes.
2. How traction and friction affect braking.
3. How weight and speed affect braking.
4. Driver reaction time and brake lag.

## The Mechanics of Stopping a Vehicle

In order for your vehicle to stop, mechanical energy must be turned into heat energy. This is done mainly through friction between the brake linings and brake drums. Friction is the force which resists movement between two surfaces in contact with each other. When you push the brake pedal in a moving vehicle, you are causing friction. You cause a surface that is not revolving with the wheel (the brake linings), to move against a surface that is revolving with the wheel (the brake drums). As the brake linings push against the drums, the drums heat and the wheels slow down. The harder the brake linings push against the brake drums, the quicker the wheels slow down. This movement is turning mechanical energy back into heat energy.

# Factors that Affect Braking

## Air Brakes Compared with Hydraulic Brakes

There are some similarities between air brakes and hydraulic brakes. Both have brake shoes with linings and brake drums that are attached to the wheels. When you push the brake pedal, the brake shoes, with their linings, move up against the brake drum and create friction which enables you to slow or stop the vehicle. What goes on between the brake pedal and the brake shoes is slightly different. When your foot depresses the brake pedal of the hydraulic brake, it pushes the fluid in the brake lines to the wheel cylinders.

This fluid forces the ends of the wheel cylinders outwards pushing the brake shoes and forcing the linings against the drum. Hydraulic brakes create energy when the brake pedal is applied. On the other hand, air brakes use stored energy (air

pressure) when the brake pedal is applied. Due to the fact that greater movement of compressed air is required, air brakes respond more slowly. Therefore, air braking systems react more slowly than hydraulic braking systems because air must be compressed, but hydraulic brake fluid does not compress.

## Air-Over-Hydraulic Brakes Compared with Hydraulic Brakes

Air-over-hydraulic brake systems are applied by hydraulic fluid and use compressed air as a power source. This system has a compressor, wet tank and reservoir to store the compressed air. When you apply the brake pedal, air pressure from a service reservoir goes to a chamber which applies pressure to the hydraulic system. Air pressure assists the movement of hydraulic fluid out to the wheel cylinders

which in turn push the brake shoes out against the drums. The air-over-hydraulic system having compressed air as a power source responds more quickly when the service brakes are applied compared to the hydraulic brake system. On tractors with air brakes, there is a service and supply line that provides air to a trailer with an air brake system.

## Several Factors that Affect How Well the Brakes on Your Vehicle Work

THEY ARE:
- friction and brake fade
- vehicle weight and speed
- traction
- proper brake adjustment
- brake wear
- driver reaction time and brake lag

## Friction and Brake Fade

Engines can only produce so much power. If the engine is overworked, it overheats. Brakes also have limits.

Too much friction between the brake linings and brake drums causes the brake drums to get hot. When the brake drums overheat, they expand. This expansion moves the brake drums further away from the brake linings. The end result is that the brake linings cannot apply as much force against the brake drums and your vehicle will need more distance to stop. This is known as mechanical brake fade. Brake fade can also occur due to overheating.

## Vehicle Weight and Speed

Every vehicle has a gross vehicle weight rating (GVWR). This rating is the combined weight of the vehicle and the load it can safely carry. The brakes on your vehicle have been designed to work effectively only when your vehicle stays within the GVWR limits.

It might take as much as a minute or two for the engine to accelerate your vehicle to full driving speed. Unfortunately, you do not have that same luxury of time to stop. In an emergency, you may be required to stop immediately. Therefore, the brakes must often work up to ten times harder than the engine does. Logically, to stop a vehicle in one tenth of the time it takes to accelerate, would require a stopping power of ten times the acceleration power.

The braking power required to stop a vehicle is affected by the weight and speed of the vehicle. As the weight and speed increase, so must the braking power.

Let us say, for example, that you are driving down the road at 40 km/h. You apply the brakes and bring the vehicle to a stop. If you load the vehicle, doubling its weight, drive at the same speed and apply the same brake force, it will take twice the distance to stop that vehicle.

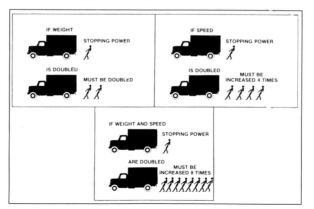

**Diagram 2-1:**
**The effects of weight and speed on brakes.**

11

# Factors that Affect Braking

Vehicle speed has an even greater impact on stopping distance. As a vehicle's speed increases, so must the braking power and/or stopping distance. If you double the speed of your vehicle, it will take you up to four times longer to stop. To stop within the same distance, approximately four times the braking power would be required.

When you double both your vehicle weight and speed, your braking power will have to be doubled for the extra weight and four times greater for the increased speed. Eight times the original braking power would now be required.

## Traction

Stopping the wheels of your vehicle and stopping your vehicle are two different things. If you combine too much brake application pressure with poor traction conditions, you may experience wheel lock-up.

Road and weather conditions, tire wear, and the weight and speed of your vehicle all affect traction. To avoid this type of wheel lock-up, you must either reduce the brake application pressure or improve traction.

Here are several tips that may help you prevent wheel lock-up:
- Keep good tread on your tires and check for proper tire inflation.
- Do not mix different construction types and sizes of tires. For example, do not mix radial and bias ply tires.
- Reduce your speed on slippery road conditions. (Keep track of weather forecasts. You cannot improve the weather, but you can be prepared for it.)
- Think ahead and whenever possible, brake sooner and apply less pressure to the brakes. Remember, a lighter brake application means you will need more time and distance to stop.

## Proper Brake Adjustment

You put yourself, the vehicle and other road users at risk if your brakes are out of adjustment. For example, if your vehicle has three axles and each of those axles has brakes attached to them on each end, each brake would be responsible for approximately 1/6th of the work needed to stop the vehicle. When properly adjusted, all six sets of brake linings should contact the brake drums at the same time. If some of the brakes are not properly adjusted, the brake linings will not push against the brake drums with the same force when you depress the brake pedal. When this happens, the properly adjusted brakes will have to work harder to make up for the improperly adjusted ones and brake fade or failure may occur.

| | Chamber Type (Square inches) | Overall Diameter | Maximum Push Rod Travel at Which Brakes Must be Readjusted |
|---|---|---|---|
| **Bolted Flange Brake Chambers** | A (12) | 6-15/16″ | 1-3/8″ |
| | B (24) | 9-3/16″ | 1-3/4″ |
| | C (16) | 8-1/16″ | 1-3/4″ |
| | D (6) | 5-1/4″ | 1-1/4″ |
| | E (9) | 6-3/16″ | 1-3/8″ |
| | F (30) | 11″ | 2-1/4″ |
| | G (30) | 8-7/8″ | 2″ |
| **Clamp Ring** | 6 | 4-1/2″ | 1-1/4″ |
| | 9 | 5-1/4″ | 1-3/8″ |
| | 12 | 5-11/16″ | 1-3/8″ |
| | 16 | 6-3/8″ | 1-3/4″ |
| | 20 | 6-25/32″ | 1-3/4″ |
| | 24 | 7-7/32″ | 1-3/4″ |
| | 24 L | 7-7/32″ | 2″ |
| | 30 | 8-3/32″ | 2″ |
| | 36 | 9″ | 2-1/4″ |
| **Rotochambers** | 9 | 4-9/32″ | 1-1/2″ |
| | 12 | 4-13/32″ | 1-1/2″ |
| | 16 | 5-13/32″ | 2″ |
| | 20 | 5-15/16″ | 2″ |
| | 24 | 6-13/32″ | 2″ |
| | 30 | 7-1/16″ | 2-1/4″ |
| | 36 | 7-5/8″ | 2-3/4″ |
| | 50 | 8-7/8″ | 3″ |

NOTE: 24 L is the long push rod stroke design.

Diagram 2-2: **Brake chamber data chart.**

Note: Improperly adjusted brakes increase stopping distance, and will affect the vehicle's parking/emergency and service brakes. Have this adjustment performed by a qualified person. Ensure that the push rod travel is checked.

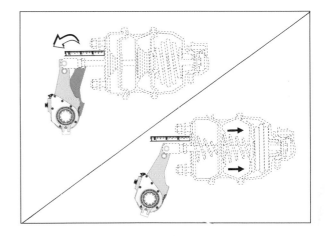

Diagram 2-3:
**Measuring push rod travel.**

13

# Factors that Affect Braking

## Brake Wear

Every time you apply your brakes, the air pressure drops. The amount of this pressure drop increases gradually as the brakes wear. Therefore, you should be familiar with the normal pressure drop which occurs on your vehicle when the brakes are fully applied after they have been adjusted. If you notice a more rapid or severe drop, you should check for the cause of the problem.

Note: Faulty valves, leaks and other problems in the air systems can also cause a drop in pressure.

## Driver Reaction Time and Brake Lag

How quickly you are able to stop depends upon how quickly you react to a braking situation. No matter how good your reflexes are, it will take you about 3/4 of a second to react. Your vehicle also needs time to react. This reaction time is known as brake lag. A typical air brake system needs approximately 4/10ths of a second for air to travel through a properly maintained air brake system after your foot presses on the brake pedal.

## Summary Questions:

1. Why do air brake systems react to a brake application more slowly than hydraulic brake systems?
2. How do weight and speed affect a vehicle's ability to stop?
3. How can you improve the traction between your vehicle's wheels and the road?
4. What happens when one or more of the brake assemblies are out of adjustment?
5. What is brake lag?

# COMPONENTS OF AN AIR BRAKE SYSTEM AND HOW THEY WORK

## Overview

This chapter contains information about:

1. Air brake system safety standards.
2. What some of the major air brake components are and how they work.
3. The service brakes compared with spring brakes.
4. How spring brakes (parking and emergency brakes) work.
5. The different types of parking brake dash control valves.

## Air Brake System Safety Standards

Your vehicle must have a service brake for normal stops, an emergency brake if the service brake fails, and a parking brake to secure the vehicle when it is parked. Also, the emergency and parking brake system has to be controlled independently of the service brake system.

In this section, we will describe the parts of the basic air brake system, what these parts look like, where they are found and how they operate.

**Note: Not every vehicle is equipped with all these parts.**

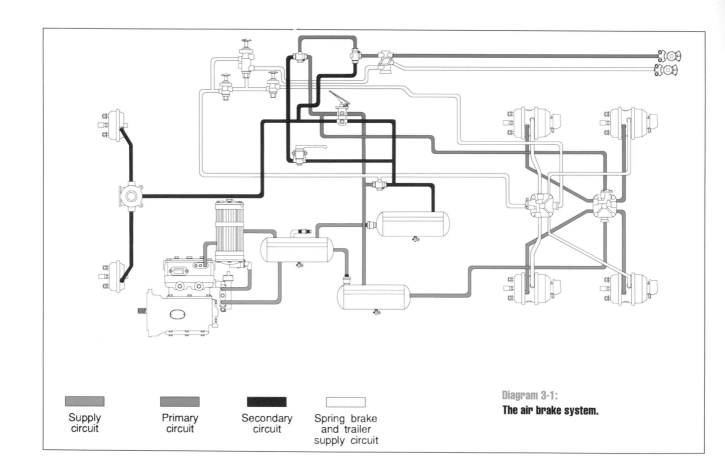

Supply circuit

Primary circuit

Secondary circuit

Spring brake and trailer supply circuit

Diagram 3-1:
**The air brake system.**

16

# Components of an Air Brake System and How They Work

## Compressor

The compressor compresses air and moves it to the wet tank (also known as the supply reservoir). The compressor is powered by the engine using either a belt or gears.

## Compressed Air

Air pressure is all around us, but because this air pressure is very slight, we simply consider it to be zero pressure. When air is compressed, it becomes warmer. This warmer air cools while in the wet tank which causes moisture and residue to separate from the air. When more air is forced into a smaller space than it would normally occupy, such as air compressed into an air tank by a compressor, air pressure is created. This pressure is usually measured in terms of kiloPascals (kPa) or pounds per square inch (psi).

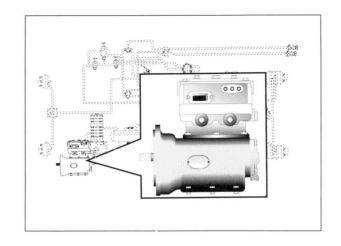

Diagram 3-2:
**The compressor pumps air into the wet tank.**

# Components of an Air Brake System and How They Work

## Governor

If a compressor pumped air continuously to the wet tank and service reservoirs, eventually the tank and reservoirs would take too much air pressure and damage would occur. When enough air enters the reservoirs and the desired level of pressure has been reached, the governor signals the compressor to cut-out and stop the flow of compressed air. Normal cut-out pressure is between 690 and 932 kPa (100 and 135 psi). As the brakes are used, compressed air leaves the reservoirs. When the pressure in the reservoir drops approximately 173 kPa (25 psi) from the maximum pressure setting, the governor will signal the compressor to cut-in and air pressure will build up in the system.

MIN.

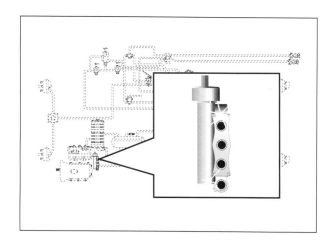

Diagram 3-3:
The governor controls when and how much air goes to the reservoirs.

Note: Some air brake systems use a simplified unloader valve instead of a governor. In a system with this valve, when maximum pressure is reached the simplified unloader valve opens, allowing air from the compressor to be vented into the atmosphere. When air pressure in the reservoir is used, the simplified unloader valve will close allowing compressed air to fill the reservoir.

## Air Dryers and Alcohol Evaporators

It is important to keep compressed air as dry as possible because water may freeze and cause brake failure. Some vehicles have an air dryer and/or an alcohol evaporator attached to the air brake system. An air dryer is located between the air compressor and the wet tank. The air dryer helps reduce the contaminants from the compressed air before it enters the wet tank. An alcohol evaporator mixes a type of alcohol into the air in the system which acts as an antifreeze. The alcohol evaporator reduces the risk of air brake valves freezing. Use only the manufacturer's recommended type of alcohol.

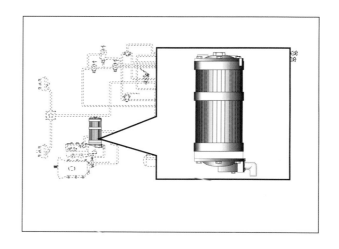

Diagram 3-4:

**The air dryer helps reduce contaminants from the air before it enters the wet tank.**

# Components of an Air Brake System and How They Work

### Safety Valve

The wet tank and air dryer on air brake equipped vehicles must have safety valves. If the governor fails and the pressure builds too high, safety valves normally open and vent air from the tank when the air pressure inside the wet tank reaches 1035 kPa (150 psi).

*MAX.*

### Wet Tank and Service Reservoirs

After the compressor compresses the air, reservoirs store it for use. The first tank is known either as a wet tank or as a supply reservoir. Most of the moisture and residue is accumulated in this tank limiting the amount sent to the service reservoirs. This moisture and residue collects at the bottom of the tank. The wet tank (supply reservoir) sends the air pressure to the service reservoirs (dry tanks), where it is stored for use.

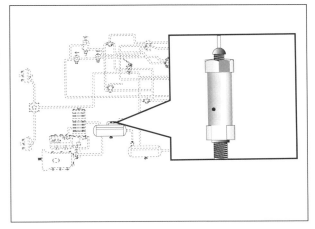

**Diagram 3-5:**
The safety valve opens and vents air pressure from the wet tank if the tank air pressure increases too much.

Note: On single circuit air brake systems, built prior to CMVSS 121, there may only be one wet tank and one service reservoir.

20

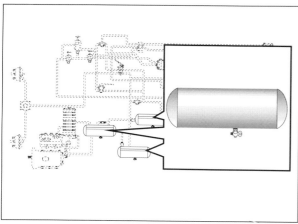

**Diagram 3-6:**

**The reservoirs store compressed air.**

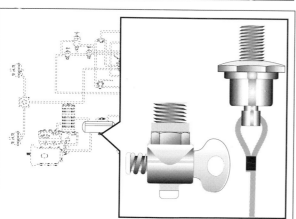

**Diagram 3-7:**

**A reservoir drain valve helps eliminate contaminants manually from the reservoirs.**

## Reservoir Draining Valves

All air tanks and/or air reservoirs have drain valves. They may be either a drain cock or a pull cord type drain valve. You may have to drain these tanks manually to allow accumulated moisture to escape. Always drain the wet tank first to help prevent moisture that has been accumulated from entering the service reservoirs. Reservoirs should normally be drained once daily; this is also an important step in the pre-trip air brake inspection.

Excessive moisture within the braking system can be dangerous because the moisture may freeze and result in brake failure.

# Components of an Air Brake System and How They Work

### (Optional) Reservoir Draining Valve

Some vehicles may have draining valves, called spit valves, that work automatically. Heaters may be attached to the spit valves to keep them from freezing. The automatic draining valves may not eliminate all contaminants.

**Note: The tank and reservoirs should be drained manually to help eliminate contaminants that may have entered the air tank and reservoirs.**

### Excessive Drain off

Any excessive oil that is noticed when draining the reservoirs should be reported. High oil usage by the compressor not only pollutes the braking system, but indicates a problem with the compressor. This oil mixes with moisture in the wet tank and forms a milky white substance which can seriously restrict the flow of air through the system.

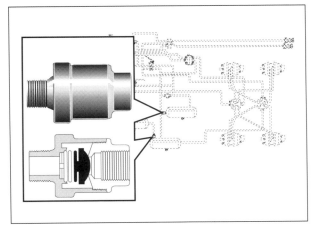

Diagram 3-8:

**The one-way check valve keeps compressed air flowing in one direction only and stops air from flowing back through the valve.**

### One-way Check Valves

The one-way check valves allow the air pressure to flow in one direction only and stop air from flowing back through the check valve. A one way check valve is attached to the inlets of the service reservoir(s).

Therefore, if a leak were to occur in the wet tank, the service reservoir(s) would not lose air pressure until a service brake application is made.

# Gauges and Warning Devices

## Air Supply Pressure Gauge

The air pressure gauge measures the amount of air pressure in the service reservoirs. On a dual circuit system there will be either one gauge for each of the two reservoirs, or one gauge with two needles to measure each reservoir's air pressure separately. All air brake equipped vehicles must have a supply pressure gauge in working order.

## Application Pressure Gauge

Some vehicles have an application pressure gauge. It shows the amount of air pressure being applied to the service brake chambers. On a tractor towing a trailer it measures air pressure to the trailer when the hand valve is applied. Hand valves will be explained in the next chapter.

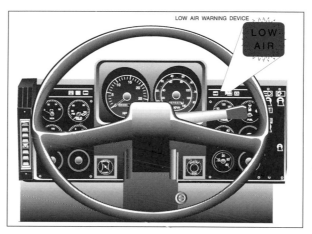

LOW AIR WARNING DEVICE

LOW AIR

Diagram 3-9:
**The low air warning devices will light up and may be audible as well when air pressure in the brake system is too low.**

**Note: Some vehicles have a warning device called a wig wag. When air pressure is too low, the arm drops into the driver's view.**

## Low Air Pressure Warning Devices

These devices must be visual and may be audible as well, that indicate when the air pressure in the brake system is dangerously low. If your service reservoir's air pressure drops to less than 414 kPa (60 psi), a red warning light should light up and/or warning buzzer may sound. When this happens, you should come to a safe stop as soon as possible. If you ignore the low air pressure warning device and fail to stop, the air pressure may drop to a level where the spring brakes apply. This will leave you with little or no control over your vehicle.

# Gauges and Warning Devices

### Foot Valve (Brake Pedal)

The brake pedal controls air pressure applied to the brakes. As you push down on the brake pedal, air from the service reservoirs is released through the foot valve toward the brake chambers where the actual braking action begins. The pressure on the foot valve controls the amount of air pressure released from the reservoirs to the chambers. This air pressure is converted into mechanical force at the brake assembly.

The more foot pressure, the further the foot valve opens, releasing more air pressure from the reservoir. The maximum air pressure available for braking is determined by the air pressure stored in the reservoir.

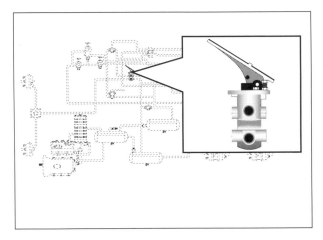

Diagram 3-10:

**The foot valve controls air pressure during a brake application.**

### Front Brake Limiting Valve

Some trucks are equipped with a front brake limiting valve. The two types used are as follows:

**Automatic -**

Which reduces the amount of air pressure to the front brakes when the foot valve is applied.

**Manual -**

This type uses a dash control valve to operate the front wheel limiting valve in wet road position. In dry road position no limiting of air pressure will occur to the front brakes.

24

## Relay Valve

The relay valves installed near the rear axle work to reduce brake lag by allowing air pressure to reach the rear brake chambers at the same time as the front brake chambers. The relay valve is used on a bus, truck, or tractor to apply and release the service brakes. They are air operated, fast response control valves. When signal air pressure from the brake pedal is sensed, it will release air pressure from the reservoir(s) to the brake chamber. When the service brakes are released, the relay valve will vent air through the quick release part of the relay valve.

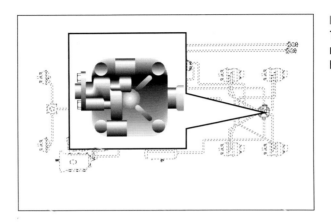

Diagram 3-11:

**The relay valve works to reduce brake lag during a brake application.**

# Gauges and Warning Devices

## Quick Release Valve

After a brake application, air pressure is exhausted from the system. When you release the brake pedal, the pressurized air will leave the brake system through the quick release valve. A quick release valve speeds up the venting of pressurized air from the brake chambers. Therefore, pumping of brakes wastes air. A quick release valve may be built into other valves.

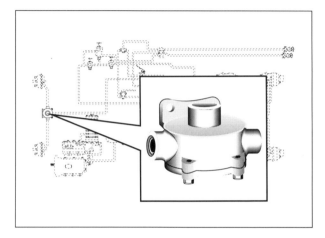

Diagram 3-12:
**The quick release valve helps vent application air pressure from the system faster.**

## Service Brake Chamber

The service brake chambers are round metal containers where air under pressure is converted into mechanical force. When you push the brake pedal, pressurized air from the service lines enters the brake chambers.

Within the brake chamber there is a flexible diaphragm, a push rod plate and a return spring. As the air fills the chamber, it pushes the push rod out to the applied position. When air pressure is released, the push rod is returned by a spring inside the chamber.

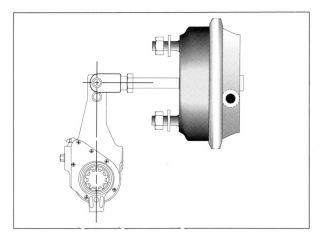

**Diagram 3-13a:**
An external view of a service portion of the brake chamber.

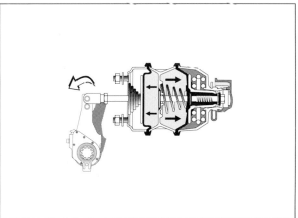

**Diagram 3-13b:**
The brake chamber converts air pressure into mechanical force.

27

# Gauges and Warning Devices

## Slack Adjuster

Slack adjusters and push rods link the brake chamber to the brake assembly.

When the push rod extends from the brake chamber, it pushes the slack adjuster. The slack adjuster's motion transfers to the brake assembly causing the brake shoes to move towards the brake drums or rotors.

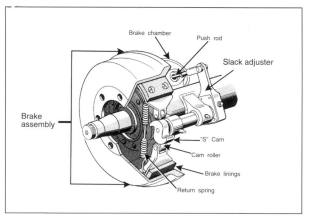

Brake chamber
Push rod
Slack adjuster
Brake assembly
"S" Cam
Cam roller
Brake linings
Return spring

**Diagram 3-14a:**
**The slack adjuster takes the mechanical force from the brake chamber and transfers it to the brake assembly.**

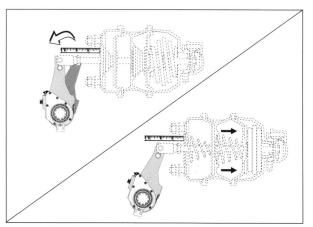

**Diagram 3-14b:**
**The slack adjusters, in the applied and released position.**

# Brake Assemblies

The brake assembly and the brake drums make up the last section of the entire air brake system. There are three types of brake assemblies:

## "S" Cam Brakes

The diagram shows the "S" cam brake assembly. It gets its name from the pointed "S" that sits between the brake shoes and is turned by the slack adjuster and cam shaft. The turning "S" forces the brake shoes and linings outward against the brake drums.

## "Wedge Brakes"

Another type of brake assembly is the "wedge" brake. Instead of turning an "S", the push rod forces a small wedge between two brake shoe rollers. The wedge forces the brake shoes and linings out against the brake drums.

**Diagram 3-15:**
**The "S" cam brake uses a cam shaped like an "S" on one end to force the brake shoes against the brake drums.**

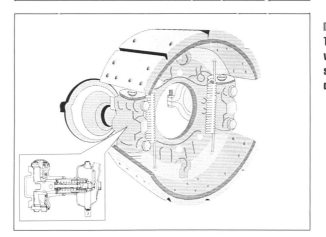

**Diagram 3-16:**
**The wedge brake uses a wedge to force the brake shoes against the brake drums.**

29

# Brake Assemblies

## "Disc Brakes"

The third type of brake assembly is the "disc" brake. It has calipers and pads on both sides of the disc. The cam shaft acts as a power screw that clamps the pads against the disc.

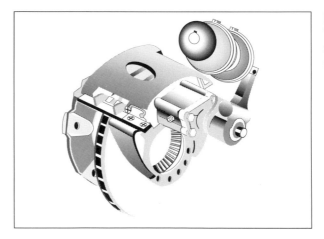

Diagram 3-17:
The disc brake uses a caliper and disc pads to clamp a rotating disc.

# Spring Brakes Compared with Service Brakes

In the service brake system, the diaphragm in the brake chamber is held back by a return spring. When the brake pedal is pushed, air pressure pushes the diaphragm against the pressure plate and spring which pushes out the push rod and moves the slack adjuster to the applied position.

In a spring brake chamber, a diaphragm, pressure plate and a powerful spring are held in the released position by air pressure. When you apply the parking brakes, air pressure leaves the spring brake chamber. The powerful spring then pushes the pressure plate which pushes the push rod and moves the slack adjuster to the applied position.

NOTE: spring brakes are usually held in the released position by air pressure and applied by spring pressure. Service brakes are applied by air pressure and released by spring pressure.

## Mechanically Released

Most types of parking brakes can be released mechanically by "winding them off" or "caging" them. A bolt, which runs through the center of the chamber body, is turned to compress the spring. Caging means the parking brakes are being released.

NOTE: There will be no parking or emergency braking action, if the spring brakes have been manually caged. Only a qualified person should manually cage the spring brake chambers, as a temporary measure, in order to move a vehicle to a safe location in an emergency situation.

WARNING: Spring brake assemblies should only be serviced by qualified personnel. These springs are under extreme pressure and could cause serious personal injury.

# Spring Brakes Compared with Service Brakes

## Spring Brakes as Parking/Emergency Brakes

Spring brakes are mechanically applied, not air applied and are designed to work when you are parking your vehicle or when your service brakes fail. Unlike service brakes, spring brakes apply when air pressure leaves the chambers and release when air pressure builds back up in the chamber.

Spring brakes can also act as emergency brakes. If the air pressure in the brake system drops, the spring brakes will apply automatically. In this case you may lose the ability to make a controlled stop. When this occurs, most dash mounted emergency control valves will automatically close which in turn will stop the flow of air. The effectiveness of the parking/emergency brakes depends on the adjustment of the service brakes. To test the effectiveness of the parking/emergency

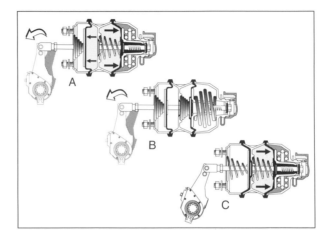

Diagram 3-18:
A. The service brake applied. B. The spring brake applied. C. The service and spring brake released.

brakes, engage a low gear and attempt to move the vehicle.

**Note: The emergency application is explained further in Chapter 5.**

# The Parking Brake Dash Control Valves

When parking your vehicle, control valves are used. The valves are operated with either a push/pull knob or a lever type control valve. The parking brake dash control valve directs air from the service reservoir to the spring brakes. Vehicles built to CMVSS 121 will be equipped with a two way check valve that allows the higher air pressure to be directed to the parking brake control valve(s) from either the primary or secondary reservoir. Therefore, the emergency brakes will not automatically apply, if a loss of air pressure were to occur in only one reservoir.

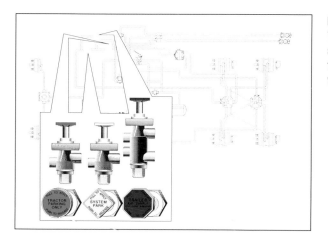

Diagram 3-19:
The tractor parking brake, system park brake and trailer air supply control valves.

## There Can Be Three Knob Arrangements

- The first is a three valve system. Usually a blue knob controls the valve for parking the tractor only. A yellow knob controls the valve for parking both the tractor and the trailer system park brake. The trailer air supply knob is red and controls the air supply to the trailer(s) being towed.

- The second is a two valve system. Like the three valve system, it usually has a yellow knob and a red knob but does not have the blue knob. Dash control valves will vary among manufacturers and vehicle models.

# The Parking Brake Dash Control Valves

Diagram 3-20:

**Lever type parking brake control valve.**

■ The third is a single parking brake control valve used in most straight trucks and buses. There will be either a push/pull knob or a lever type parking brake control valve.

## Summary Questions

1. What are the low pressure warning devices?
2. What is the difference between the service brake and the spring brake?
3. Why do you drain the wet tank first?
4. Air pressure causes the service brakes to apply. What causes the spring brakes to apply?
5. What are the differences between the three different dash control valves?
6. What is the purpose of the air dryer?
7. An air pressure gauge shows how much air is in what?
8. What is the function of the governor?
9. What is the purpose of the one-way check valve?
10. How much application pressure can be applied to air brakes?

# DUAL CIRCUIT AIR BRAKE SYSTEMS

## Overview

This chapter contains information about:

1. The difference between a single and dual circuit air brake system.
2. What the major components of a dual circuit system are and how they work.
3. The advantage of a dual circuit system over a single circuit system.

## Dual Circuit Air Brake Systems

The dual circuit air brake system might seem complicated, but if you understand the basic air system and, if the dual system is separated into its basic functions, it becomes quite simple.

The dual system is two systems or circuits in one. There are different ways of separating the two parts of the system. On a two-axle vehicle, one circuit operates the rear axle and the other circuit operates the front axle. If one circuit has a failure, the other circuit will continue to operate.

Note: All air line diagrams are used to illustrate basic dual circuit air brake system principles only and are not to be interpreted as regulations for, or specifications of, dual air brake systems.

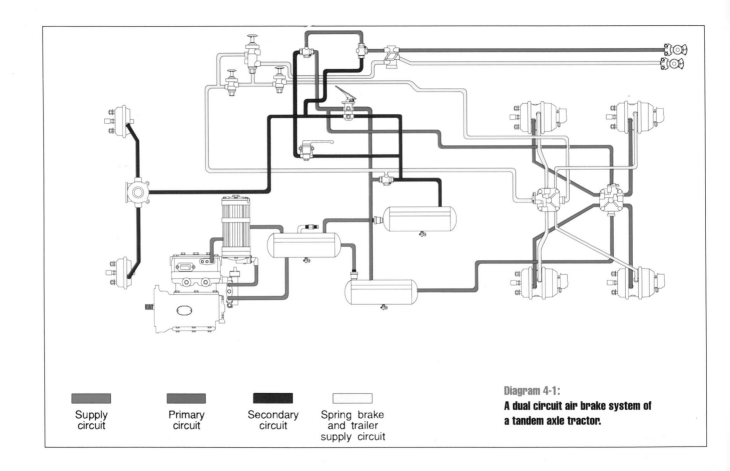

Supply
circuit

Primary
circuit

Secondary
circuit

Spring brake
and trailer
supply circuit

**Diagram 4-1:**

**A dual circuit air brake system of a tandem axle tractor.**

36

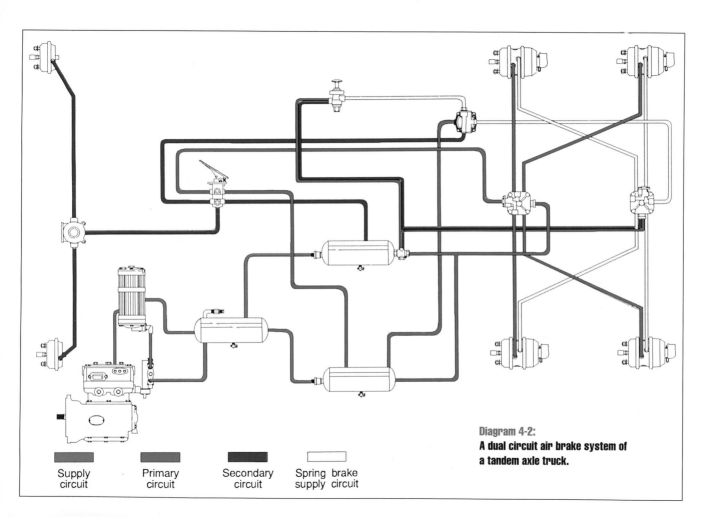

**Supply circuit**  **Primary circuit**  **Secondary circuit**  **Spring brake circuit**

Diagram 4-2:
A dual circuit air brake system of a tandem axle truck.

37

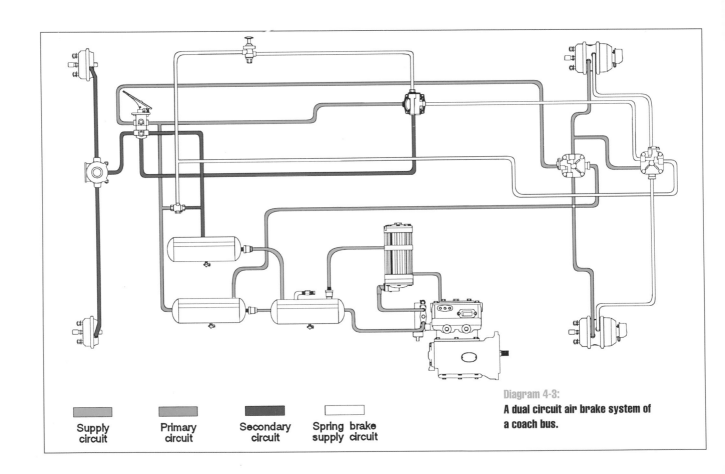

Diagram 4-3:

**A dual circuit air brake system of a coach bus.**

Supply circuit

Primary circuit

Secondary circuit

Spring brake supply circuit

# Dual Circuit Air Brake Systems

In diagrams 4-4 and 4-5, air is pumped by the compressor to the wet tank which is protected from over pressurization by a safety valve. Pressurized air moves from the "wet" supply tank to the primary reservoir (green) and the secondary reservoir (red) through one-way check valves. Air from the primary reservoir is directed to the foot valve. Air is also directed from the secondary reservoir to the foot valve. The foot valve is similar to the one described earlier in the Single Circuit Air Brake System, but has been divided into two sections (two foot valves in one).

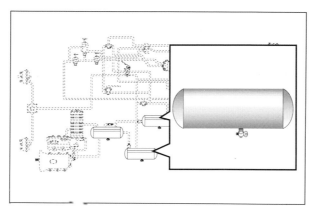

**Diagram 4-4:**
**The primary and secondary service reservoirs provide air pressure to separate axles.**

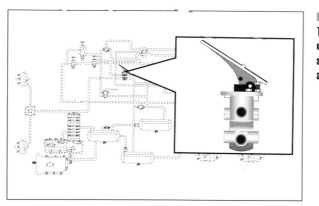

**Diagram 4-5:**
**The dual circuit foot valve controls the primary and secondary service brake application.**

39

# Dual Circuit Air Brake Systems

One section of this dual foot valve controls the primary circuit and the other section controls the secondary circuit. When a brake application is made, air is drawn from the primary reservoir (green) through the foot valve and is passed on to the rear brake chambers. At the same time, air is also drawn from the secondary reservoir (red), passes through the foot valve and is passed on to the front brake chambers. If there is an air loss in either circuit, the other circuit will continue to operate independently. Unless air is lost in both circuits, the vehicle will continue to have braking ability. Both the primary and secondary circuits are equipped with low pressure warning devices and pressure gauges. If the low air warning comes on, the driver should bring the vehicle to a safe stop at the earliest opportunity.

## Modulating Valve

Some vehicles are equipped with a modulating valve that will perform a unique safety function. This modulating valve controls the spring brakes in the event of a service system failure by releasing air from the spring brake chambers when the foot valve is applied. The air released is equal to the amount of air applied by the foot valve. This application from the spring brake chamber will be limited to the amount of force produced by the spring.

## Summary Questions

1. What are the advantages of a dual air brake system?
2. Locate the primary and secondary reservoir on the diagrams in this chapter. Where do they receive their air from?

# TRAILER AIR BRAKE SYSTEM

## Overview

This chapter contains information about:

1. How service and spring brakes work on trailers.
2. What the major trailer air brake components are and how they work.

## Trailer Air Brake System

So far you have read about an air brake system as it applies to a bus, truck or tractor. The air brake system of a trailer is similar. The brake system in a trailer has at least one reservoir, two brake lines, brake chambers and brake assemblies with brake linings and drums. However, the compressed air servicing the trailer must be supplied by the tractor's compressor. This chapter will explain what goes into a trailer's air brake system, and how it works.

# The Tractor Protection System

This is an important part of the tractor's air system that supports the trailer's air brake system. It has two valves that work with each other. They are the trailer air supply and tractor protection valves.

## Trailer Air Supply Valve

The trailer air supply valve is mounted on your tractor's dash, is usually red and has eight sides like a stop sign. When the valve is closed, the tractor's compressor will supply air only to the tractor's air tanks. When it is open, the compressor will fill both the tractor's and trailer's air reservoir(s). When the trailer's air brake system is working correctly, the trailer's air pressure should be the same as the tractor's air pressure.

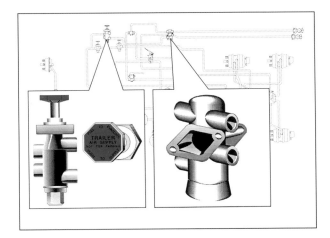

Diagram 5-1:
The tractor protection system is the trailer air supply valve and the tractor protection valve.

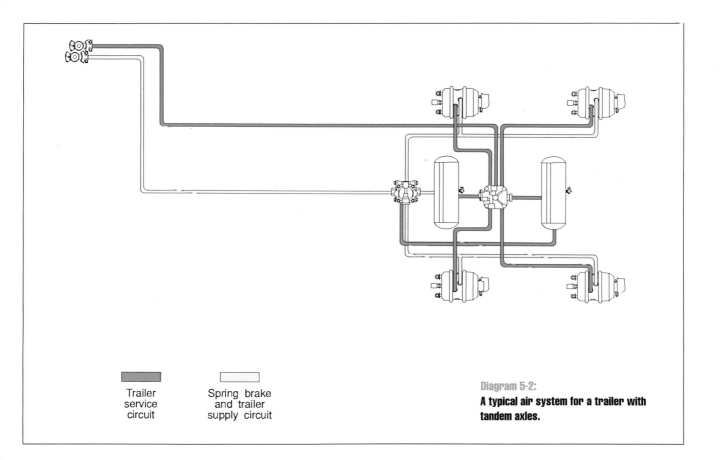

Trailer
service
circuit

Spring brake
and trailer
supply circuit

Diagram 5-2:

**A typical air system for a trailer with tandem axles.**

43

# The Tractor Protection System

## Tractor Protection Valve

The function of the tractor protection valve is to open and close the air lines to the trailer. The purpose of the tractor protection valve is to protect the tractor's air pressure in the event of rapid air loss from the trailer. Therefore, if the trailer reservoir(s) were to lose the air pressure, the tractor's service reservoir(s) should drop to approximately 138 to 311 kPa (20-45 psi), the tractor protection valve will close, and the trailer emergency brakes will apply immediately. This keeps your tractor's service brakes working if the tractor protection valve closes.

Two ways to check the operation of the tractor protection valve with the system at maximum pressure and the "trailer emergency brakes" released are as follows:

1. Disconnect the supply line. The trailer emergency brakes should apply.

There should be no air pressure loss from the trailer gladhand. Check the low air warning device(s) signal at 414 kPa (60 psi) minimum. The power unit air pressure should hold between 311-138 kPa (45-20 psi) when the tractor protection valve closes. Some systems may hold at higher pressures.

WARNING: Use caution when disconnecting the supply line. The system is at maximum pressure.

2. Disconnect the service line. No air should escape or leak from the tractor or trailer gladhands. Make a service brake application. The low air pressure warning device(s) signal at 414 kPa (60 psi) minimum. The tractor air pressure will drop to 311-138 kPa (45-20 psi). The tractor protection valve will close, trailer brakes should apply and tractor air loss from the service line should cease.

## Foot Valve

When a truck or tractor with air brakes is towing a trailer equipped with air brakes, the foot valve or brake pedal controls the brakes of a truck or tractor and the trailer.

## Hand Valve

The hand valve controls the air pressure to the trailer service brakes. With the hand valve, you may apply as much or as little air pressure to the trailer service brakes as you wish. The hand valve of a tractor-trailer unit is not to be used for parking. Because most hand valves do not lock, they may return to the inactive position without warning.

## Two-Way Check Valve

The two-way check valve allows air to be directed to one delivery line from one of two sources. A two-way check valve allows the source applying the higher pressure to shift the shuttle so that the higher pressure will be directed to the delivery or "service line". A two-way check valve allows the trailer service brakes to operate should there be a failure in either the primary or secondary system. A two-way check valve is used between the foot and hand valve, for the purpose of independently controlling the trailer service brakes.

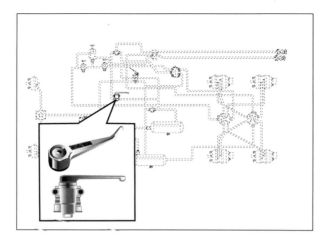

**Diagram 5-3:**
**The hand valve controls the service brake application to the trailer.**

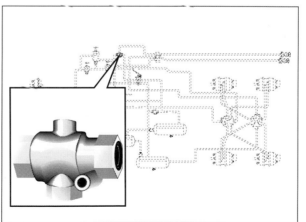

**Diagram 5-4:**
**The two-way check valve directs air pressure from the foot valve or the hand valve to the trailer.**

# The Tractor Protection System

### AIR LINES: Service Line

The service line is the air line that sends an air pressure signal used by the service brakes during a brake application. It connects the foot valve and hand valve of the truck or tractor with the trailer's service braking system. When you apply the foot or hand valve, the service line sends air pressure in the form of a signal that opens the trailer relay valve and releases air pressure to the brake chambers. If this service line ruptures, loss of control of the trailer service brakes will result when a service brake application is made. If enough air is lost, the tractor protection valve will close and the trailer emergency brakes will apply. If the service line is colour coded, it will usually be blue.

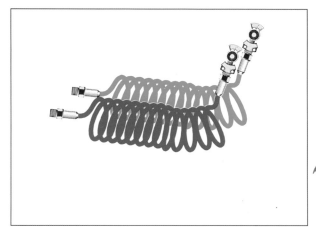

Diagram 5-5:

**The flexible air lines on the back of the truck/tractor connect the supply and service lines from the truck/tractor to the trailer.**

90° ELBOW
NEED 7 MEETER
HOSE

### AIR LINES: Supply Line

The other line is known as the supply line or the emergency line. The supply line provides a path from the reservoirs of the tractor/truck to the trailer's air reservoir(s).

If there is a loss of pressure in the trailer supply line, you would expect the trailer brakes to be applied and the tractor/truck brakes to remain operable. When it is colour coded, it will usually be red.

## GLADHANDS (Hose Couplers)

You will find gladhands at the end of the service and supply air lines from the truck or tractor and at the front of the trailer. Each has a rubber seal to keep air pressure from escaping when you connect them together. Many tractors and trailers will have special fitting "polarized" gladhands designed so that they only match with the correct "polarized" trailer gladhands, but polarized gladhands can be incorrectly coupled to non-polarized couplers.

### Connecting the Air Lines

To connect the truck or tractor air system to the trailer air system, you snap-lock the truck or tractor's glad-hands with the trailer's gladhands. Start by lining up the two rubber seals between the truck/tractor and trailer and have the gladhands at a 90 degree angle to one another. Twist the top gladhand down and

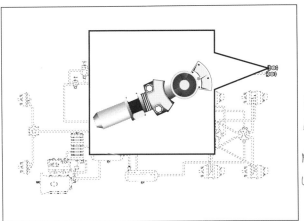

**Diagram 5-6:**

**The gladhands (hose couplers) are the connecting devices on the end of the supply and service air line.**

POLORIZED TO POLORIZED WILL NOT MIX UP

POLORIZED TO UNPOLORIZED
UNPOLORIZED TO POLORIZED
MAY MIX UP

this will secure the connection. If you cross the supply line and the service line, the trailer brakes will not release. Remember, the blue hose is for the service line and the red hose is for the supply or emergency line.

### Storing and Cleaning the Gladhands

Most trucks/tractors have a protection plate or "dead end couplers" that gladhands attach to when they are not being used. Make sure the gladhands are clean before connecting them. Storing and cleaning the gladhands will help keep dirt and water from getting into the trailer's air system.

47

# Trailers Built Prior to CMVSS 121 Standards

These trailers were not required to have mechanically applied parking brakes. Instead, they use air brake chambers as an "emergency system". The air pressure in the supply air line controls the "emergency system". A trailer using air brake chambers as an "emergency system" can be hooked to tractor/truck and other trailer(s) with spring brake chambers as their "emergency system". A trailer with air brakes must have at least one service reservoir which supplies air to the trailer braking system.

## Relay Emergency Valve

Once air pressure travels from the tractor/truck through the service and supply lines, it passes through to the trailer's relay emergency valve. It directs air from the trailer reservoir to the trailer brake chambers when you apply the service or parking brakes. The relay emergency valve automatically closes and directs the air pressure from the reservoir to the trailer brake chambers when there is an emergency such as a break in the supply air line. This causes the "trailer emergency system" to apply. The emergency relay valve also acts as a one way check valve which stops air pressure in the trailer from flowing back to the tractor/truck. The quick release portion of the valve vents/exhausts the air pressure after the brakes are released.

# Trailers Built to CMVSS 121 Standards

Trailers with air brakes are now required to have a mechanically applied "parking/emergency system" that operates independently of the service system.

Also trailers must have at least two reservoirs. Trailer service reservoirs get their air pressure from the supply air line. The trailer's service reservoir(s) stores compressed air. There are two basic valves used with the spring brake system. They are as follows:

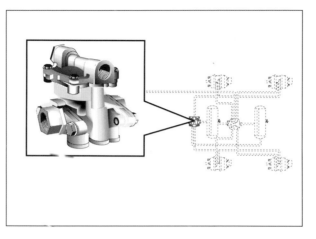

Diagram 5-7:

**The trailer spring brake valve controls both the parking/emergency brakes and acts as a one-way check valve.**

## Spring Brake Valve

A trailer spring brake valve allows air to pass directly to the spring brake chambers. When air enters the one way check/pressure protection part of the spring brake valve it will open allowing air to fill the trailer tanks. A sudden loss of air in the supply system causes the trailer spring brake valve to vent/exhaust the air from the trailer spring brake chamber, applying the trailer spring brakes. The spring brake valve also acts as a one way check valve which stops air pressure in the trailer from flowing back to the tractor/truck.

# Trailers Built to CMVSS 121 Standards

## Relay Valve

The relay valve(s) is similar to the relay valve mentioned in chapter 3. This valve applies the trailer service brakes when the hand valve or brake pedal is applied. When the service brakes are released, the relay valve will vent air through the quick release part of the relay valve.

## Summary Questions

1. With the system at full pressure, what will happen to your tractor and trailer if the trailer supply (emergency) line breaks?
2. With the system at full pressure, what will happen to your tractor and trailer if the service line to the trailer breaks?
3. What is the difference between the foot valve and the hand valve?
4. Should you use the hand valve for parking?

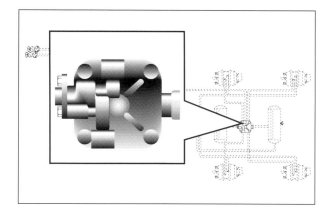

Diagram 5-8:

The trailer relay valve acts as a relay valve and a quick release valve.

5. If the service and supply lines are colour coded, what will their colours be?
6. Can gladhands be incorrectly connected?
7. Why are tractors equipped with a tractor protection valve?

# AIR BRAKE PRE-TRIP INSPECTION

## Overview

This chapter contains information about:

1. Inspection Requirements.
2. Air Brake Pre-Trip Inspection (Bus, Truck or Tractor).
3. Air Brake Pre-Trip Inspection (Combination Vehicles).
4. Automatic Emergency System Test (Dual System Power Units).

## Inspection Requirements

The pre-trip inspection/circle check in the Air Brake Handbook acts as a guide for anyone intending to drive a motor vehicle equipped with air brakes. It also allows student drivers to suitably prepare themselves for a Ministry air brake ("Z" endorsement) examination(s). The legal requirement for a commercial motor vehicle pre-trip inspection is covered in the Highway Traffic Act, Regulation 575.

# Air Brake Pre-Trip Inspection (Bus, Truck or Tractor)

The air brake pre-trip inspection is designed to help you identify potential air brake problems prior to driving the vehicle. This is to inform you of items you will be expected to know and/or demonstrate, for your air brake practical examination.

(If an item does not apply to your vehicle, you will not be expected to demonstrate knowledge of that item.)

## Secure the Vehicle
1. Park your vehicle on level ground.
2. Apply the dash mounted parking brake control valve.
3. Block/chock wheels (to avoid vehicle movement).

## Check Compressor
1. Check security of the compressor and belt condition and tension.
2. Check the condition and security of hoses and fittings.

## Drain the Wet Tank and Reservoirs
1. Drain the wet tank first; then check the air pressure gauge(s). There should not be any air pressure loss from the service reservoir(s).
(This will drain most of the contaminants from the wet tank and ensure that the one-way check valves are working.)
2. Manually drain each service reservoir down to zero pressure, and observe gauge after each reservoir has been drained. Only one needle of the air gauge(s) should be affected per reservoir.

## Start Engine - Build System Pressure to Maximum
1. Check that the low air warning device(s) cut out at 414 kPa (60 psi) minimum.
2. With engine RPM at 600-900 the air pressure should build from 587 to 690 kPa (85 to 100 psi) within 2 minutes.
3. The governor should cut out between 690 and 932 kPa (100 and 135 psi).
4. Release the parking brakes; measure each push rod. Check the visible portions of the brake drum for cracks; visually check the linings for condition and thickness on those assemblies with no dust plates.
5. Secure the pedal in the applied position; check and note each push rod for travel. There should be no audible air leaks from the service or supply system, and there are no brake chamber(s) manually caged.

## Stop Engine - with System at Maximum Pressure

1. Make a full foot brake application and hold for one minute. The air pressure drop in one minute should not exceed 14 kPa (2 psi) for each half of a dual circuit system.

2. Start the engine and rebuild the air pressure to maximum. With the engine running, lightly fan the service brakes by applying and releasing the brake pedal rapidly.

a. The governor should cut in when the pressure drops approximately 173 kPa (25 psi) from the maximum air pressure setting.

b. The low air warning devices should signal at 414 kPa (60 psi) minimum.

c. If equipped with spring brakes, parking/emergency spring brake application should occur between 311-138 kPa (45-20 psi) system pressure.

d. With the spring brakes applied, remove the blocks/chocks from the wheels.

e. With the system pressure to maximum, engage the lowest forward gear and the spring brakes should hold the vehicle stationary at a low engine idle; attempt to move the vehicle.

f. Release the spring brakes; move the vehicle forward slowly and apply the service brakes for response.

53

# Air Brake Pre-Trip Inspection (Combination Vehicles)

The tractor and trailer(s) should be fully connected to perform an air brake pre-trip inspection.

## Secure the Vehicle

1. Park your vehicle on level ground.
2. Apply the dash mounted parking brake control and the trailer supply/emergency valves.
3. Block/chock wheels (to avoid vehicle movement).

## Check Compressor

1. Check security of the compressor and belt condition and tension.
2. Check the condition and security of hose and fittings.

## Drain the Wet Tank and Reservoirs

1. Drain the wet tank first and then check the air pressure gauge(s) inside your vehicle cab. There should not be any air loss in the service reservoir(s). (This will drain most of the contaminants from the wet tank and ensure that the one-way check valves are working.)
2. Manually drain each service reservoir down to zero pressure and observe gauge after each reservoir has been drained. Only one needle of the air gauge should be affected per reservoir.

## Start Engine - Build System Pressure to Maximum

1. Check that the low air warning device(s) cut out at 414 kPa (60 psi) minimum.
2. With the engine RPM at 600-900, and the air supply to the trailers shut off, the air pressure should build from 587 to 690 kPa (85 to 100 psi) within 2 minutes.
3. The governor should cut out between 690 and 932 kPa (100 and 135 psi).
4. Release the tractor parking brakes and trailer emergency brakes; measure each push rod. Check the visible portions of the brake drum for cracks; visually check the linings for condition and thickness on those assemblies with no dust plates.
5. Secure the pedal in the applied position, measure and note each push rod for travel. There should be no audible air leaks from the service or supply systems, and there are no brake chamber(s) manually caged.

## Stop Engine - With System at Maximum Pressure

1. Make a full service brake application and hold for one minute. The pressure drop in one minute should not exceed:

   a. 28 kPa (4 psi) for a tractor/truck and one trailer.

   b. 41 kPa (6 psi) for a tractor and two trailers.

2. Start the engine and rebuild the air pressure to maximum. With the engine running, lightly fan the service brakes by applying and releasing the brake pedal rapidly:

   a. The governor should cut in when the air pressure drops approximately 173 kPa (25 psi) from the maximum air pressure setting.

   b. The low air warning devices should signal at 414 kPa (60 psi) minimum.

   c. The trailer brake application should occur between 311 and 138 kPa (45 and 20 psi). Tractor brake application will occur at a lower pressure.

   d. With spring brakes applied, remove the blocks/chocks from the wheels.

   e. With the system pressure to maximum, engage the lowest forward gear. The spring brakes should hold the vehicle stationary at a low engine idle; attempt to move the vehicle.

   f. Release spring brakes; move the vehicle forward slowly and apply the trailer(s) service brakes for response.

   g. Move the vehicle forward slowly and apply the brake pedal to test the total brake response on all units.

# Automatic Emergency System Check/Dual Circuit Air Brake Systems

With system at full pressure and engine stopped:

1. Drain the wet tank then drain the secondary reservoir to zero pressure:
   a. The primary reservoir should not lose pressure.
   b. On combination vehicles, the trailer air brake system should remain charged.
   c. The tractor and trailer emergency brakes should not apply automatically.
2. With no air pressure in the secondary reservoir, make a service brake application:
   a. The primary system brakes should apply and release.
   b. On combination vehicles the trailer brakes should also apply and release.
   c. The brake light(s) should activate.
3. Slowly drain the primary reservoir pressure.

   a. The tractor protection valve should close between 311 and 138 kPa (45 and 20 psi).
   b. The trailer emergency brakes should apply after the tractor protection valve closes.
   c. The spring brakes should apply between 311 and 138 kPa (45 and 20 psi).
4. Close the drain cocks (valves), recharge the system and drain the wet tank. Then drain the primary reservoir to zero kPa/psi.
   a. The secondary reservoir should not lose pressure.
   b. On combination vehicles, the trailer air brake system should remain charged.
5. With no air pressure in the primary reservoir, make a brake application:
   a. The secondary system brakes should apply and release.
   b. On combination vehicles, the trailer brakes should also apply and release.

   c. If the power unit is equipped with a modulating relay spring brake control valve, the spring braked axle(s) of the primary system should apply and release.

## Summary Questions

1. What is the first step in a pre-trip inspection?
2. Why is it necessary to drain the wet tank first?
3. How many kPa (psi) difference should there be between the cut-in and cut-out pressure of the governor?
4. Why is a pre-trip air inspection necessary?
5. At what minimum pressure should the low air warning device signal?

# BRAKING TIPS AND IDENTIFYING POTENTIAL BRAKE PROBLEMS

## Overview

In this chapter you will learn:

1. Tips for Brake Use and Performance.
2. How to Identify Potential Problems That May Occur with the Air Brake System.

While you are not expected to service the brake system, you should know how to use the brakes and identify potential brake problems.

# Tips for Brake Use and Performance

Using the brakes properly will help to increase their life and performance. The following are a few "good braking" tips.

1. Apply the brakes with steady pressure at the beginning of a stop. Reduce foot pressure as the vehicle slows. When coming to a complete stop, hold the vehicle with the service brakes.

2. For long downhill grades, select a lower gear and if braking is required, use a light steady foot brake application. This will hold air in the system. If you apply and release the brakes rapidly on a long downhill grade, too much air pressure will be lost and the brakes may overheat and you may be unable to stop the vehicle safely. If a greater application pressure is required for each brake application, it indicates brake fade due to overheated drums and/or defective linings.

3. If the low air pressure warning device comes on at any time, immediately stop the vehicle in the safest available place. The loss of air pressure must be corrected before proceeding.

4. If the service brakes fail on a level road, downshift and use the engine compression to slow the vehicle. If a shorter stopping distance is required, the vehicle's emergency/parking brakes may have to be applied by using the parking brake dash control valve. If this is necessary, be prepared for your vehicle to come to an uncontrolled stop. Do not drive the vehicle until repairs have been made by a qualified person.

5. Do not "overbrake" the vehicle on slippery surfaces or in a curve. Overbraking can result in skidding or wheel lock-up.

# How to Identify Potential Problems in Trucks, Buses, Tractors and Trailers Equipped with Air Brakes

Braking ability is affected by improperly set slack adjusters, oversize brake drums and other components.

Here are a few conditions that may help identify potential problems in the air brake system:

### 1. Excessive Compressor Cut-in

If the compressor cuts-in when the air brake system is fully charged and not using air pressure, something may be wrong with the governor or compressor.

### 2. Insufficient Brakes

Brakes need adjusting; lubrication or shoes need to be relined (brake fade).
Wrong type brake lining.
Poor fit between lining and drum.
Low air pressure.
Brake valve defective - not delivering pressure.
Incorrect brake chamber push rod travel.
Restricted air line(s).
Defective relay valve.

### 3. Brakes Apply Too Slowly

Brakes need adjusting or lubricating.
Low air pressure in the brake system.
Brake valve delivery pressure below normal.
Excessive air leakage when brakes applied.
Restricted tubing or hose line.
Binding in camshaft or anchor pins.
Binding in brake linkage.

### 4. Brakes Release Too Slowly

Brakes need adjusting or lubricating.
Brake valve not returning to fully released position.
Restricted air line(s).
Exhaust port of brake valve or quick release valve restricted or plugged.
Brake shoe return spring or brake chamber spring is weak or broken.
Defective brake valve or quick release valve.
Binding in camshaft or anchor pins.
Binding in brake linkage.

# How to Identify Potential Problems with Trailers

## 5. Brakes Grab

Grease on brake lining - reline brakes.
Brake drum out of round.
Defective relay valve.
Brake assembly binding.
Wrong type brake lining.

## 6. Uneven Brakes

Brakes need adjusting, lubricating or relining.
Grease on lining.
Brake shoe return spring or brake chamber spring is weak or broken.
Brake drum out of round.
Leaking brake chamber diaphragm.

**Note: If heavy use of the brakes requires increased foot pressure each time they are applied, the cause may be oversized drums due to overheating, defective linings, or both.**

## 1. Brakes Do Not Apply

Brake system not properly connected to brake system of truck/tractor.
Tractor protection valve malfunctioning.
No air pressure - trailer supply valve not releasing.
Plugged air line(s).

## 2. Brakes Do Not Release

Brake system not properly connected to towing vehicle.
Relay-emergency valve in emergency position.
Tractor protection valve malfunctioning.
Faulty quick release valve.

## Summary Questions:

1. What should you do if your brakes fail on level ground?
2. How can you tell if there is a problem in the compressor or the governor?
3. What are some problems that could cause slow brake application?
4. What could cause trailer brakes not to apply?
5. What are some causes of uneven braking?

# CONVERSION CHART

| kPa | PSI | kPa | PSI | PSI | kPa | PSI | kPa |
|---|---|---|---|---|---|---|---|
| 5 | ¾ | 300 | 43 | 1 | 6.9 | 60 | 414 |
| 10 | 1 ½ | 350 | 51 | 2 | 13.8 | 65 | 449 |
| 15 | 2 ¼ | 400 | 58 | 3 | 20.7 | 70 | 483 |
| 20 | 3 | 450 | 65 | 4 | 28 | 75 | 518 |
| 25 | 3 ½ | 500 | 72 | 5 | 34.5 | 80 | 552 |
| 30 | 4 ¼ | 550 | 80 | 6 | 41.4 | 85 | 587 |
| 35 | 5 | 600 | 87 | 7 | 48.3 | 90 | 621 |
| 40 | 5 ¾ | 850 | 94 | 8 | 55 | 95 | 655 |
| 45 | 6 ½ | 700 | 101 | 9 | 62.1 | 100 | 690 |
| 50 | 7 ¼ | 750 | 109 | 10 | 69 | 105 | 725 |
| 60 | 8 ¾ | 800 | 116 | 15 | 103 | 110 | 759 |
| 70 | 10 | 850 | 123 | 20 | 138 | 115 | 794 |
| 80 | 11 ½ | 900 | 130 | 25 | 173 | 120 | 828 |
| 90 | 13 | 950 | 138 | 30 | 207 | 125 | 863 |
| 100 | 14 ½ | 1000 | 145 | 35 | 242 | 130 | 897 |
| 150 | 22 | 1050 | 152 | 40 | 276 | 135 | 932 |
| 200 | 29 | 1100 | 159 | 45 | 311 | 140 | 966 |
| 250 | 36 | | | 50 | 345 | 145 | 1000 |
| | | | | 55 | 380 | 150 | 1035 |

# Glossary of Terms

**AIR DRYER:** An in-line filtration system that removes both liquid and water vapour from the air that is discharged from the compressor before it reaches the wet tank.

**AIR PRESSURE COMPRESSED AIR:** Air which has been forced into a smaller space than that which it would ordinarily occupy in its free or atmospheric state.

**ALCOHOL EVAPORATOR:** This device adds vaporized alcohol into the air brake system. The usage of a manufacturer's specified type of air brake antifreeze is recommended. The alcohol evaporator will help prevent freezing in the braking system when a vehicle is operated in below freezing temperatures.

**BLOCK (CHOCK):** Wood, metal or rubber blocks placed in front and behind the tires to prevent movement of the vehicle.

**BRAKE FADE:** A loss of a vehicle's effective braking power. This can be caused by improperly fitted brake shoes, water or oil on the brake linings, or excessive heat in the brake drum(s).

**CONVERTER DOLLY:** The converter dolly is a triangular shaped towing device with a fifth wheel and an axle. You use a converter dolly when pulling multiple trailers.

**DEAD END COUPLER:** A coupling device used to protect the tractor's gladhands from dirt and water when not in use. This is sometimes referred to as "Dummy Couplers".

**DUST SHIELD:** A shield or plate that covers the brake assembly.

**EMERGENCY BRAKES:** The emergency brake is a brake that is used if the service brakes fail. Some emergency brakes are manually operated by the driver, but most operate automatically.

**FANNING BRAKES:** This refers to applying and releasing the service brakes rapidly.

**FRONT BRAKE LIMITING VALVE:** This reduces the amount of air pressure to the front brakes when the foot valve is applied.

# Glossary of Terms

**GLADHANDS:** They are couplers attached to the air hoses used to connect the tractor or truck's air lines to the trailer.

**LEVER TYPE PARKING BRAKE CONTROL VALVE:** This valve requires the driver to switch the control to either the parking brake on or off position.

**PARKING BRAKES:** The parking brakes are the brakes which are used when parking your vehicle. On vehicles built after 1975, this brake will usually be applied by a mechanical spring brake.

**RESERVOIR:** A reservoir serves the air brake system as a storage area for a volume of compressed air pressure.

**SINGLE CIRCUIT AIR BRAKE SYSTEM:** The single circuit system uses one source of air supply to be used as a parking, emergency and service brake system.

**SPRING BRAKE CHAMBER, SERVICE PORTION:** This portion operates the service brakes of the vehicle. They are applied by air pressure and released by spring pressure.

**SPRING BRAKE CHAMBER, SPRING CHAMBER PORTION:** This chamber applies the parking and emergency brakes of the vehicle. They are applied by spring pressure and released by air pressure.

**TANK:** See Reservoirs.

# Index

# List of Diagrams

# Acknowledgements

The Ministry of Transportation of Ontario would like to give special thanks to the following for their assistance in the technical and written content of the handbook:

- Markel Institute of Professional Transport Training
- Proco Transportation Services Inc.

# Other Official Handbooks for You

Copies of this handbook and others may be purchased from a retail store near you, from a Driver Examination Office, from a Vehicle Licence Issuing Office or from the distributor.

Distribution:

**General Publishing Co. Limited**
30 Lesmill Road,
North York,
Ontario M3B 2T6

or by calling
(416) 445-3333 ext. 616
or 1 (800) 387-0141

Prepayment required by cheque or credit card — VISA or Mastercard

The Official Driver's Handbook $ 7.95
ISBN 0-7778-4463-X

The Official Motorcycle Handbook $ 7.95
ISBN 0-7778-3887-7

The Official Off-Road Vehicles Handbook $ 4.95
ISBN 0-7778-4456-7

The Official Truck Handbook $ 7.95
ISBN 0-7778-4454-0

The Official Bus Handbook $ 7.95
ISBN 0-7778-4452-4

The Official Air Brake Handbook $ 12.95
ISBN 0-7778-4450-8

All prices are subject to 7% G.S.T. and 5% Shipping Costs. Please add 12% to your total purchase to cover G.S.T. and shipping cost.

# STOP! Did you know there are other books in the official driver information series?

Now you can purchase copies of this official handbook and five others from a retail store, a Driver Examination Office or a Vehicle Licence Issuing Office near you—or you can order them directly from the distributor.

Distribution: **General Publishing Co. Limited**
30 Lesmill Road, North York, Ontario M3B 2T6
or by calling (416) 445-3333 ext. 616 or 1-800-387-0141 Fax (416) 445-5967

Prepayment required by cheque or credit card — VISA or Mastercard

---

**QUANTITY**

| | | | TOTAL |
|---|---|---|---|
| _____ | ISBN 0-7778-4463-X  The Official Driver's Handbook | $  7.95 | _____ |
| _____ | ISBN 0-7778-3887-7  The Official Motorcycle Handbook | $  7.95 | _____ |
| _____ | ISBN 0-7778-4456-7  The Official Off-Road Vehicles Handbook | $  4.95 | _____ |
| _____ | ISBN 0-7778-4454-0  The Official Truck Handbook | $  7.95 | _____ |
| _____ | ISBN 0-7778-4452-4  The Official Bus Handbook | $  7.95 | _____ |
| _____ | ISBN 0-7778-4450-8  The Official Air Brake Handbook | $  12.95 | _____ |
| | | Sub-Total | ___ _ |
| | | Plus 12% | _____ |
| | | TOTAL | _____ |

All prices are subject to 7% G.S.T. and 5% Shipping Costs. Please add 12% to your total purchase to cover G.S.T. and shipping cost.

Payment by          cheque ☐          VISA ☐          Mastercard ☐

Credit Card No. _____  Expiry Date _____

Signature of Card Holder _____

**SHIP TO (PLEASE PRINT):**

Name: _____

Address: _____

Town/City: _____

Province: _____  Postal Code: _____

# ONTARIO TRANSPORTATION MAP Series—including the Official Road Map of Ontario

Get a more detailed look at specific areas of Southern Ontario with this series of eight maps, scaled at 1:250,000. You'll find enlargements of major city centres, highways, townships, municipal roads including loose surface and seasonal roads, railways, airports, parks, O.P.P. detachments, hospitals, tourist attractions and service centres within each region.

Or pick up the Official Road Map of Ontario, which shows all of Ontario's highways and major roads.

Purchase your maps now at retail outlets across Ontario, or order them directly from the distributor.

## General Publishing Co. Limited
30 Lesmill Road, North York, Ontario  M3B 2T6  Telephone (416) 445-3333 OR 1-800-387-0141  Fax (416) 445-5967

Prepayment required by cheque or credit card VISA or Mastercard.

---

| QUANTITY | | | | TOTAL |
|---|---|---|---|---|
| _____ | Map #1 | Southwestern Ontario | $  7.00 | _____ |
| _____ | Map #2 | Lake Huron - Georgian Bay Area | $  7.00 | _____ |
| _____ | Map #3 | Manitoulin Island | $  7.00 | _____ |
| _____ | Map #4 | Central Ontario | $  7.00 | _____ |
| _____ | Map #5 | South Central Ontario | $  7.00 | _____ |
| _____ | Map #6 | Upper Ottawa Valley | $  7.00 | _____ |
| _____ | Map #7 | Eastern Lake Ontario | $  7.00 | _____ |
| _____ | Map #8 | Eastern Ontario | $  7.00 | _____ |
| _____ | | Complete Set of 8 (for the price of seven) | $  49.00 | _____ |
| _____ | | Official Road Map of Ontario | $  2.95 | _____ |
| _____ | | Provincial Highway Distance Table (highway distance in kilometres) | $  7.95 | _____ |

All prices are subject to G.S.T., P.S.T. and shipping costs. Please add 20% to your total purchase to cover taxes and shipping costs.

Sub-Total _____
Plus 20% _____
TOTAL _____

Payment by        cheque ☐        VISA ☐        Mastercard ☐

Credit Card No. _____        Expiry Date _____

Signature of Card Holder _____

**SHIP TO (PLEASE PRINT):**

Name: _____

Address: _____

Town/City: _____

Province: _____        Postal Code: _____

# EXPRESS YOURSELF

## with graphic licence plates for as low as $52.10.

To order, or for more information,
visit your local *Driver and Vehicle Licence Office* or call

## 1-800-AUTO-PL8  (1-800-288-6758)

Gift certificates available

© MLBP 1995   © NHL Enterprises, Inc. 1995   © 1995 NBA Properties Inc.   © CFL Properties